PRE - NURSERY

ENVIRONMENTAL STUDIES

DREAMLAND PUBLICATIONS
J-128, Kirti Nagar, New Delhi - 110 015, India
Tel. : +91-11-2510 6050, 2543 5657
E-mail : dreamland@dreamlandpublications.com
Shop online at www.dreamlandpublications.com
Follow us on www.instagram.com/dreamland.publications

Published in 2026 by
DREAMLAND PUBLICATIONS
J-128, Kirti Nagar, New Delhi - 110 015, India
Tel. : +91-11-2510 6050, 2543 5657
E-mail : dreamland@dreamlandpublications.com
www.dreamlandpublications.com

ISBN : 978-93-5089-929-8

Contents

MYSELF

Paste your photograph.

NO ONE LOOKS THE WAY I DO
NO ONE TALKS THE WAY I DO
NO ONE WALKS THE WAY I DO
I KNOW I AM SPECIAL
AND THAT IS REALLY TRUE

Date: ________________ Teacher's Signature: ________________

DO WE GROW WITH AGE?

Paste pictures of yourself.

1 YEAR OLD

2 YEARS OLD

3 YEARS OLD

Date: ________________

Teacher's Signature: ________________

THAT'S ME

Complete the following answers to introduce yourself.

Q1. What is your name?

Ans. My name is ____________________________

Q2. Are you a boy or a girl?

Ans. I am a ____________________________

Q3. Which school do you go to?

Ans. I go to ____________________________ school.

Q4. What is your teacher's name?

Ans. My teacher's name is ______________________

Q5. Where do you live?

Ans. I live in ____________________________

Q6. Which is your favourite fruit?

Ans. My favourite fruit is ______________________

Q7. Which is your favourite colour?

Ans. My favourite colour is ______________________

Date: ____________ Teacher's Signature: ____________

MY BODY

This is my body. My body has many parts.
Read the names of parts of my body.

Eye

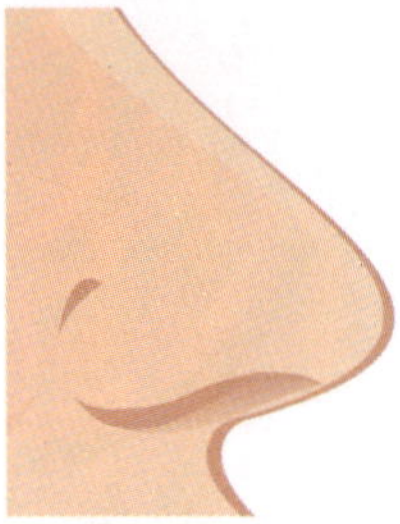

Nose

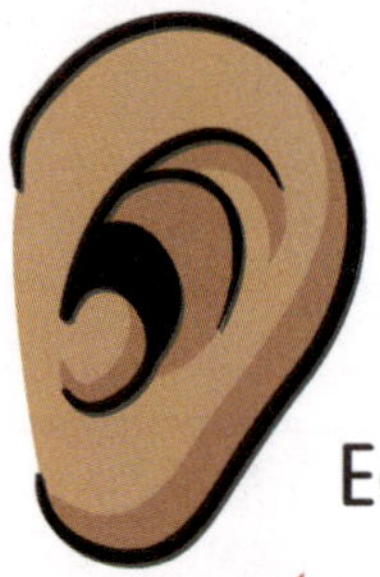

Ear

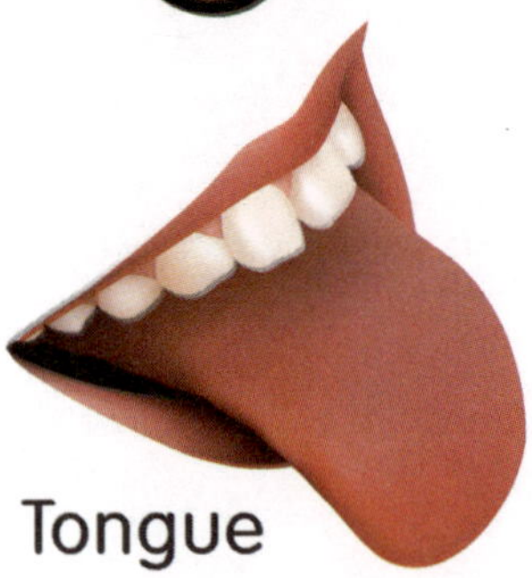

Tongue

Hand

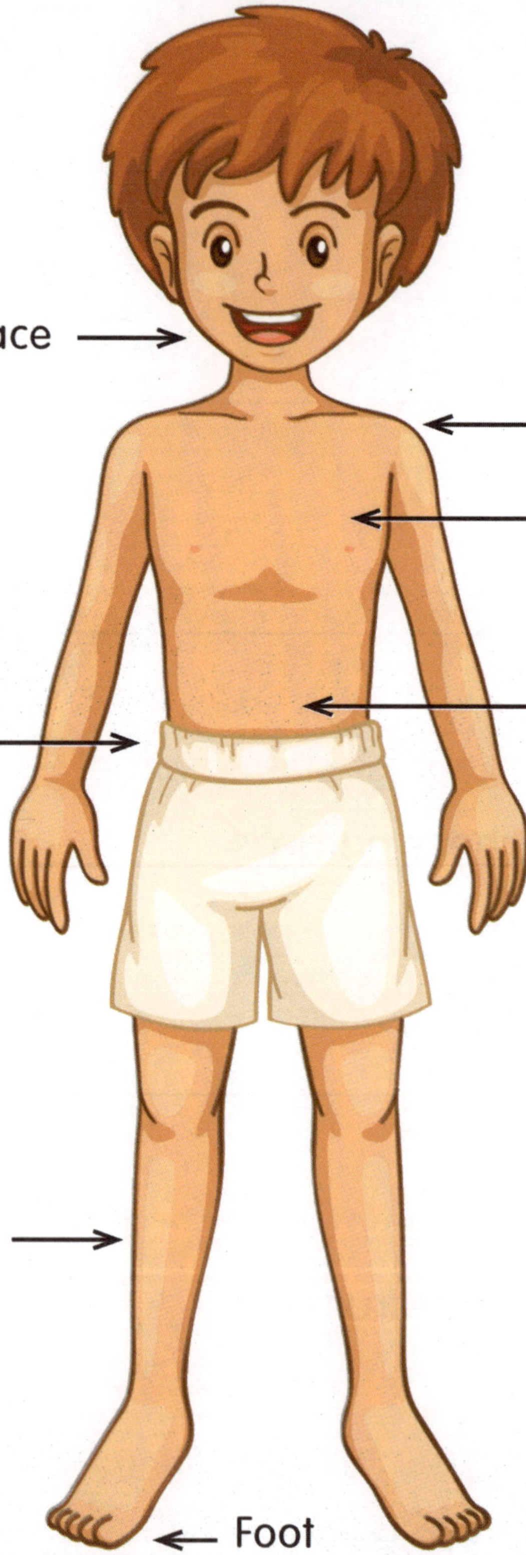

Date: ________________ Teacher's Signature: ________________

MY BODY PARTS

Date: ____________________

Teacher's Signature: ____________________

CIRCLE TIME

Which of these are parts of your body?
Circle them.

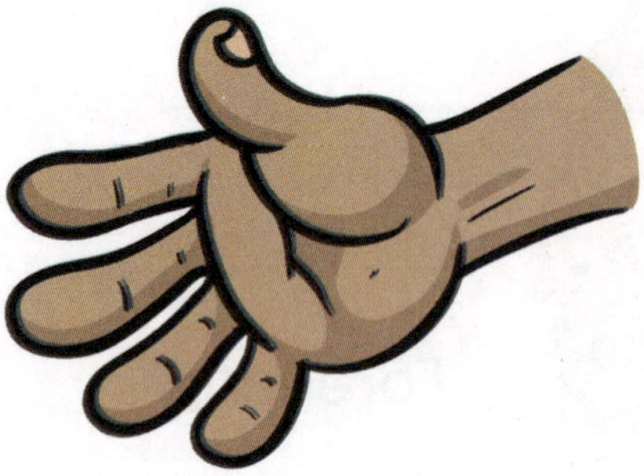

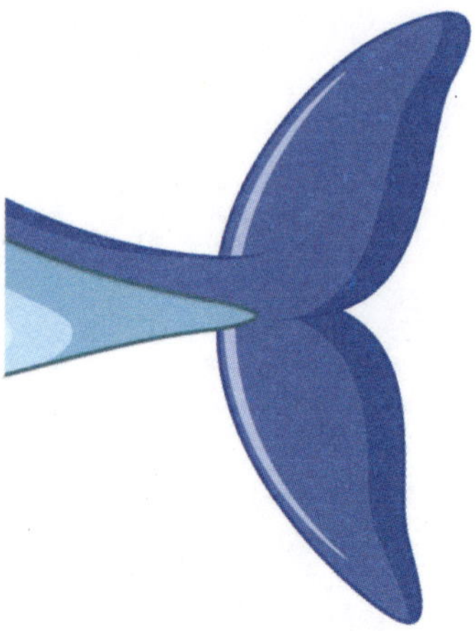

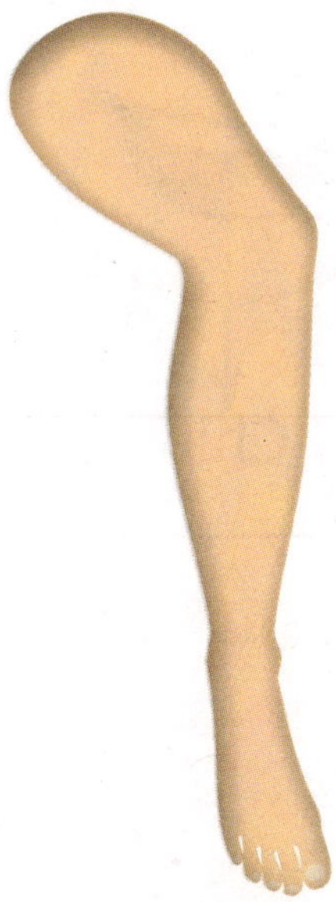

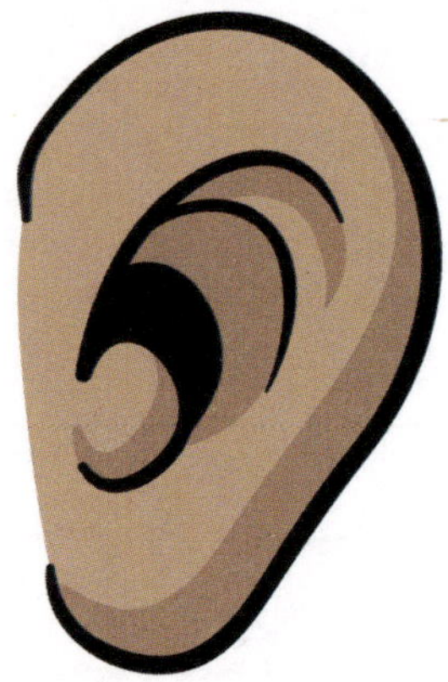

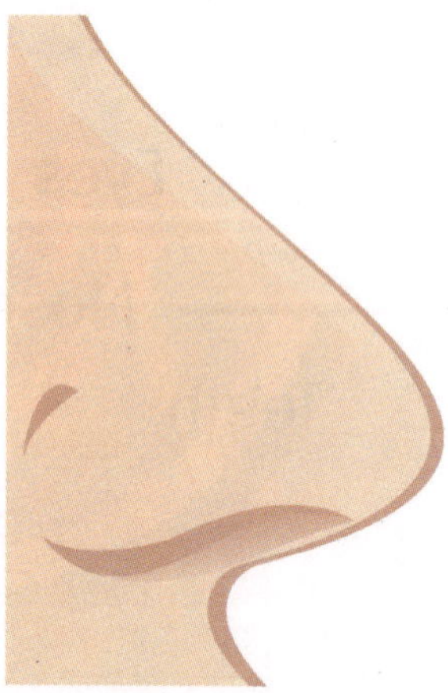

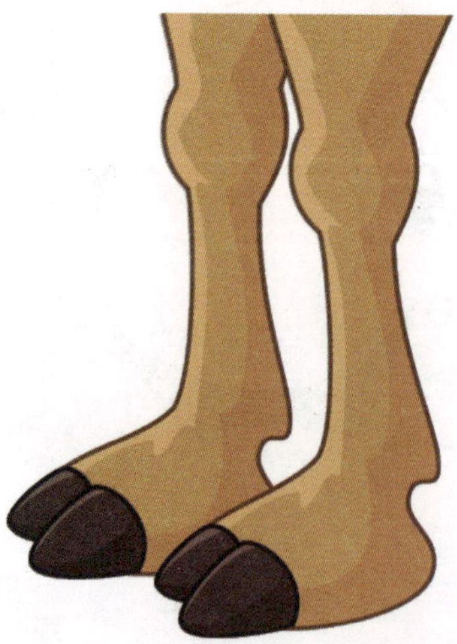

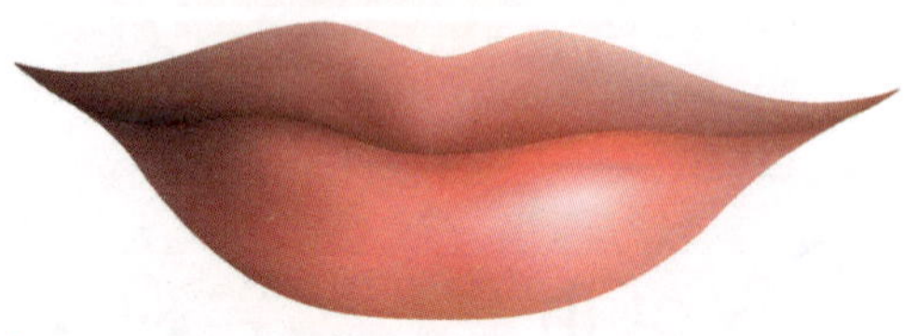

Date: ________________

Teacher's Signature: ________________

MY WONDERFUL BODY

Each part of my body performs different functions.

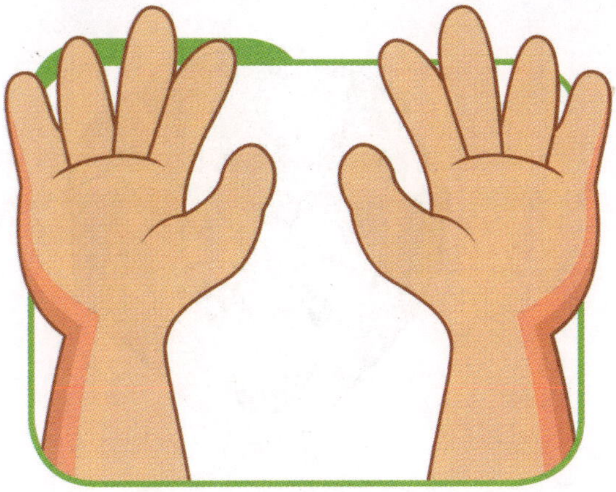

Hands are to touch and work with. My hands help me to hold, push and lift things. They help me to write.

Feet are to stand, walk and run on. My feet help me to walk, run, jump or kick. I stand on my feet.

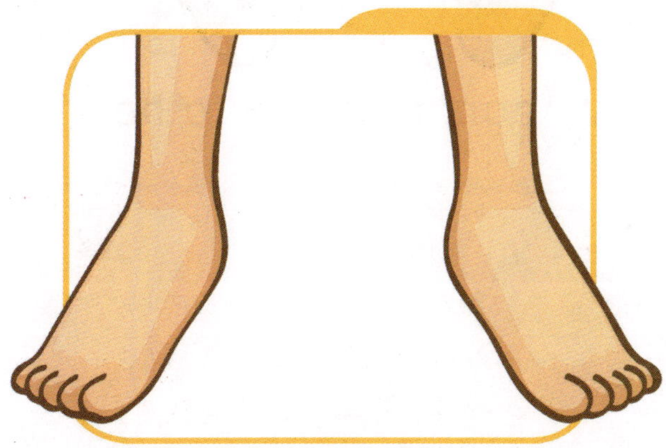

My wonderful body parts help me do these activities.

Date: ________________ Teacher's Signature: ________________

MY SENSE ORGANS

Eyes, Ears, Nose, Tongue, and Skin are my five sense organs.

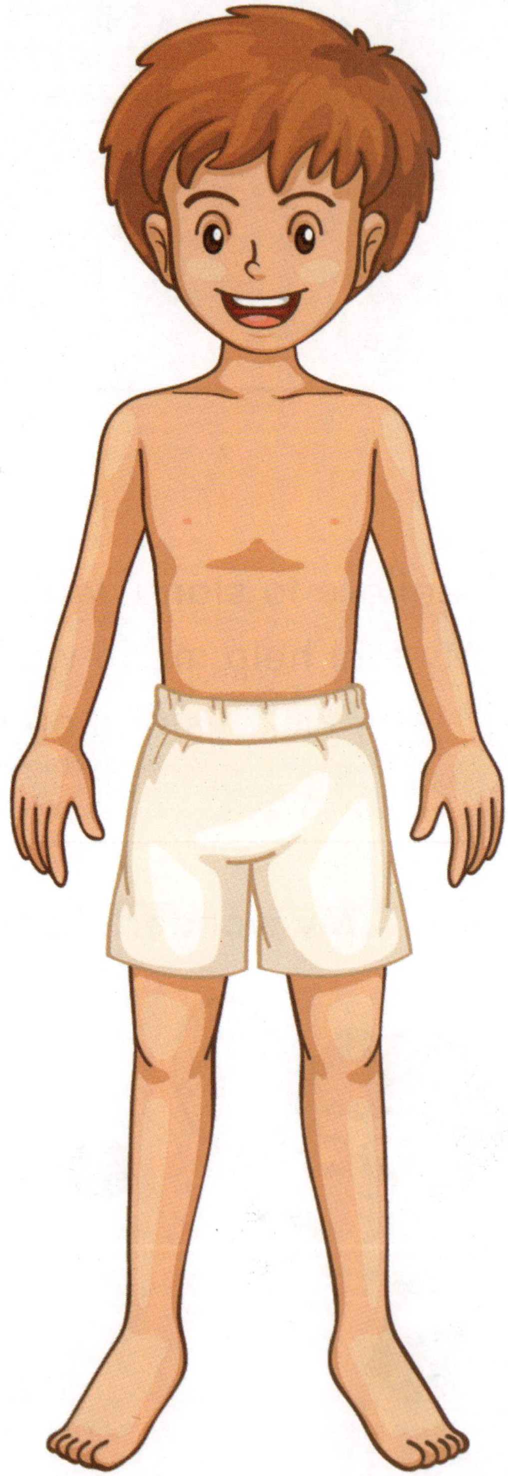

Two eyes help me to see things.

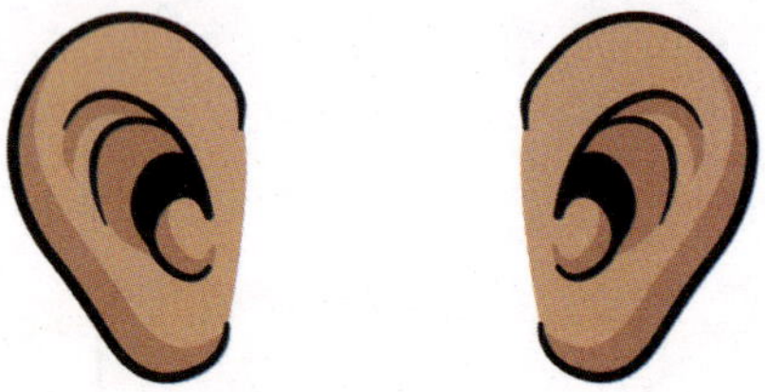

Two ears help me to hear sounds.

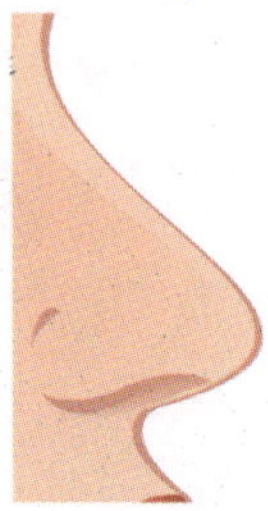

One nose helps me to smell and breathe.

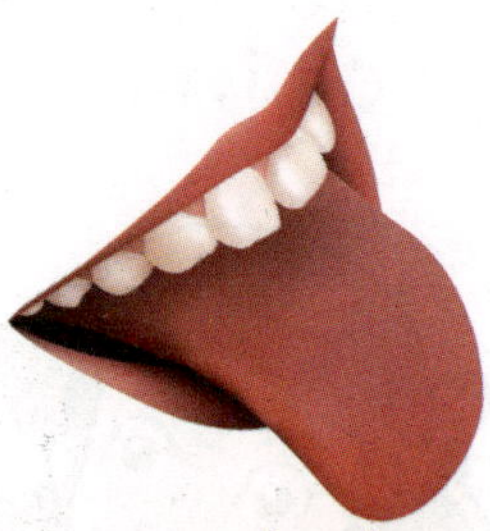

One tongue helps me to taste food.

My skin helps me to feel.

Date: ______________ Teacher's Signature: ______________

MATCH YOUR FIVE SENSES

Which sense organ goes best with each picture?

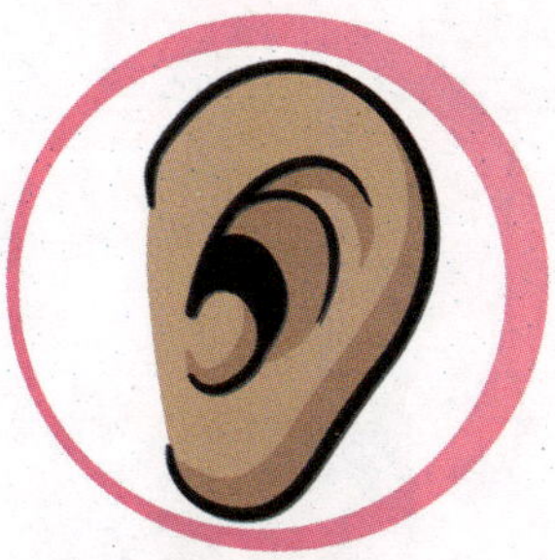 

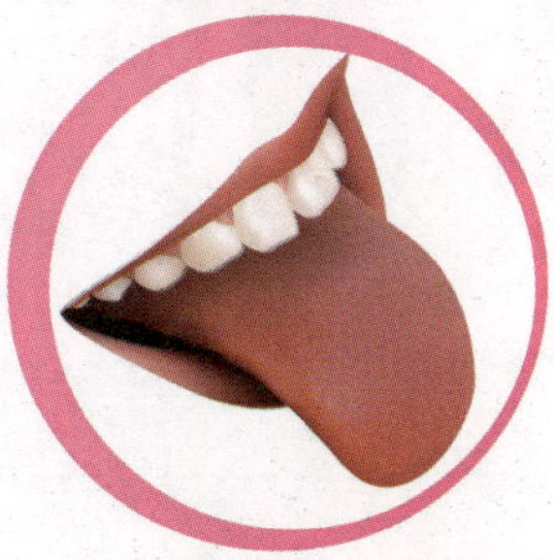 

Date: ____________________ Teacher's Signature: ____________________

MEET MY FAMILY

We live together. We love one another.

Date: ________________

Teacher's Signature: ________________

MY FAMILY MEMBERS

Draw a line to match the family members to their names.

Sister

Mother

Brother

Grandmother

Father

Grandfather

Date: ________________

Teacher's Signature: ________________

PICTURE PASTING

Paste pictures of your family members in this house.

Date: ________________ Teacher's Signature: ________________

MY FAMILY

Complete the following answers
to introduce your family.

Q1. What is your father's name?

Ans. My father's name is ______________________

Q2. What is your mother's name?

Ans. My mother's name is ______________________

Q3. What is your brother's or sister's name?

Ans. My brother's/sister's name is ______________________

Q4. Who cooks food for you?

Ans. My ______________________ cooks for me.

Tick who belong to your family.

Date: ______________ Teacher's Signature: ______________

GOOD HABITS

We should take care of our body.

Brush your teeth twice a day.

Take bath daily.

Eat healthy food.

Comb your hair daily.

Date: ______________

Teacher's Signature: ______________

LET'S RECITE

Read aloud a rhyme on my body parts.

TWO LITTLE 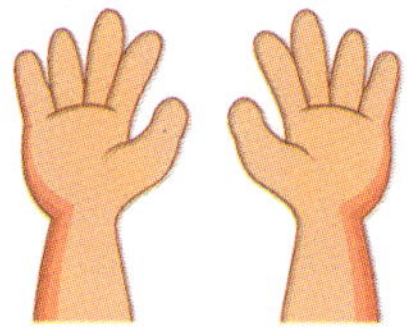 HANDS

GO CLAP - CLAP - CLAP

TWO LITTLE FEET 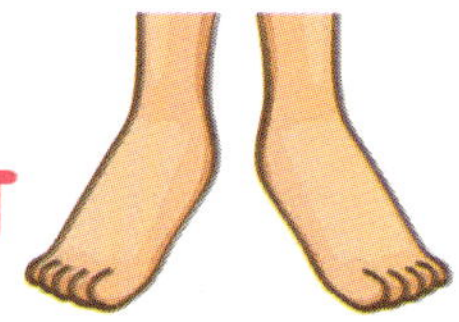

GO TAP - TAP - TAP

TWO LITTLE 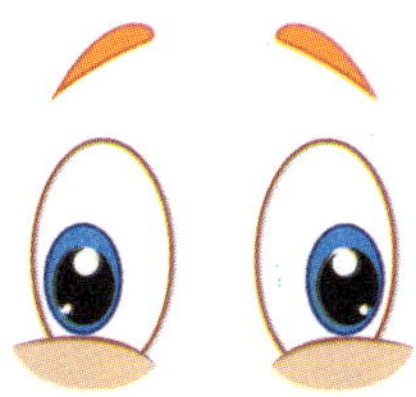 EYES

ARE OPENED WIDE

ONE LITTLE HEAD 

GOES SIDE TO SIDE

Date: ________________

Teacher's Signature: ________________

Tick (✓) the good habits and cross (X) the bad habits.

Date: ______________

Teacher's Signature: ______________

MY SCHOOL

Meet Us At School!

LEARN NEW WORDS

School, Classroom, Teacher, Students, Playground

Date: ________________ Teacher's Signature: ________________

MY CLASSROOM

Name the things that
you see in the classroom.

LEARN NEW WORDS

Teacher, Students, Books, Blackboard
Chalk, Table, Chair, Desk, Dust bin

Date: ________________ Teacher's Signature: ________________

THINGS IN MY CLASS

Circle and Colour the things
that you use in the classroom.

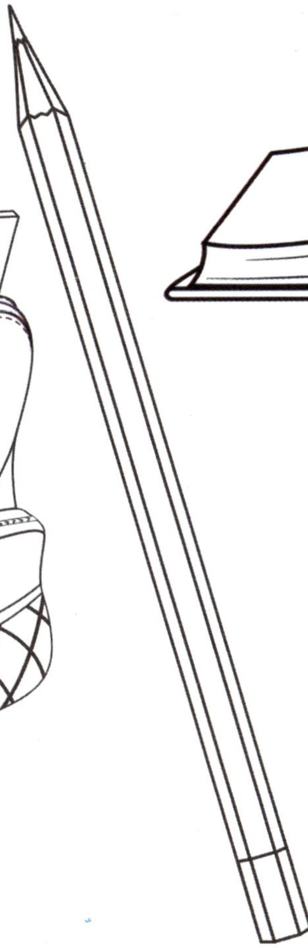

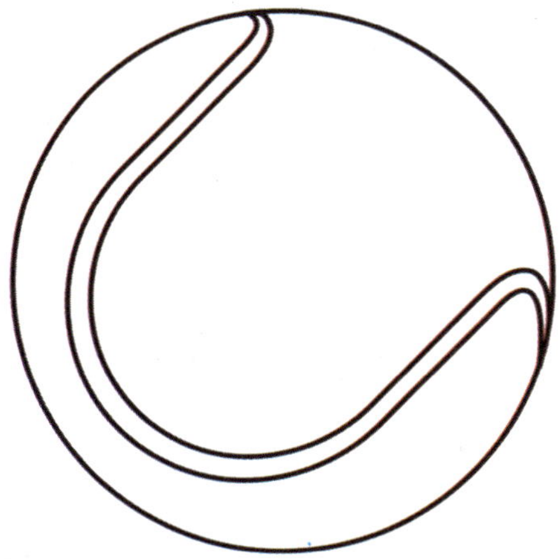

Date: ________________

Teacher's Signature: ________________

MY SCHOOL BAG

Paste the pictures of things that you carry in your school bag.

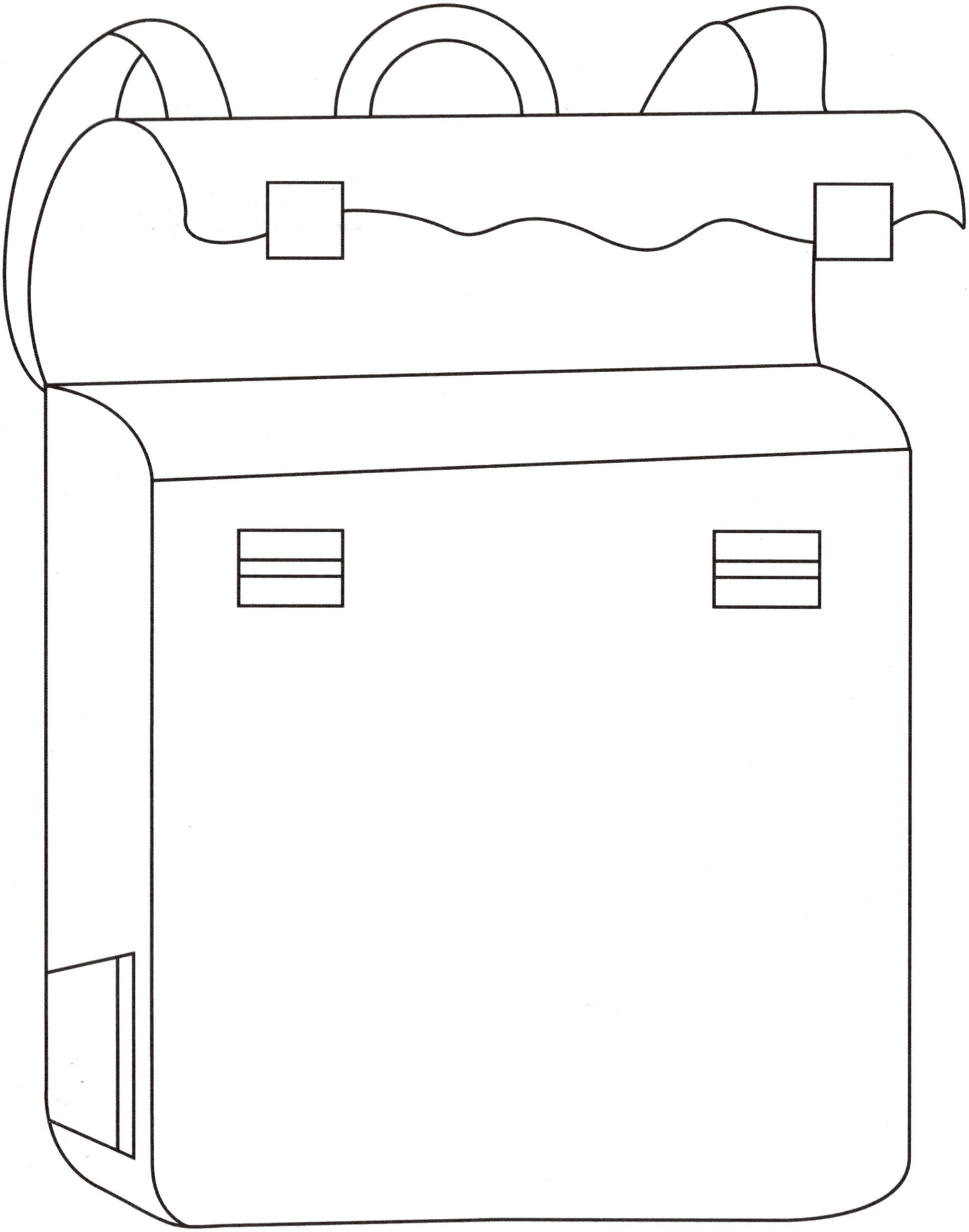

Date: ________________ Teacher's Signature: ________________

BACK TO SCHOOL

Complete the following answers about your school.

Q1. What is the name of your school?

Ans. The name of my school is ________________

Q2. What is your teacher's name?

Ans. The name of my teacher is ________________

Q3. How do you come to school?

Ans. I come to school by ________________

Q4. What all do you see in your classroom?

Ans. I see ________________________________ in my classroom.

Q5. Where do you throw the waste in the classroom?

Ans. I throw the waste in the ______________

Q6. Match us with our pictures.

Ans. teacher blackboard desk

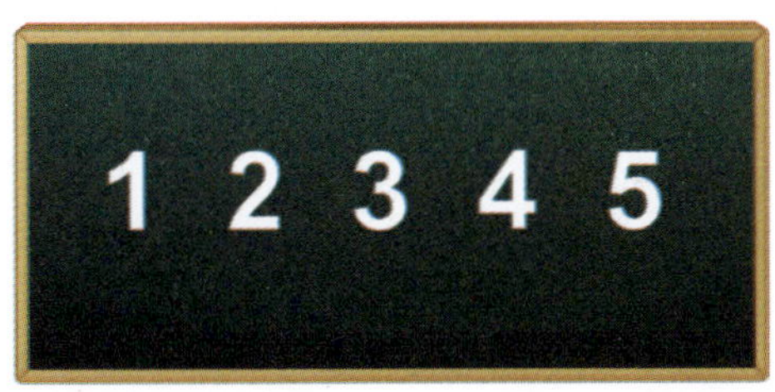

Date: ________________

Teacher's Signature: ________________

FOOD

When we are hungry we eat food. We eat many types of food.

We eat bread, butter, cheese, rice.

We eat fruit and nuts.

We eat green vegetables, fruits and vegetables to make us healthy.

Some people eat meat, fish and eggs.

We also have tea, coffee, milk, lemonade, juice, etc.

Date: ________________ Teacher's Signature: ________________

WE EAT FOOD

Colour the things that we eat.

Date: ________________ Teacher's Signature: ________________

HEALTHY FOOD

Circle the food that is healthy.

Fruits

Vegetables

Cheese

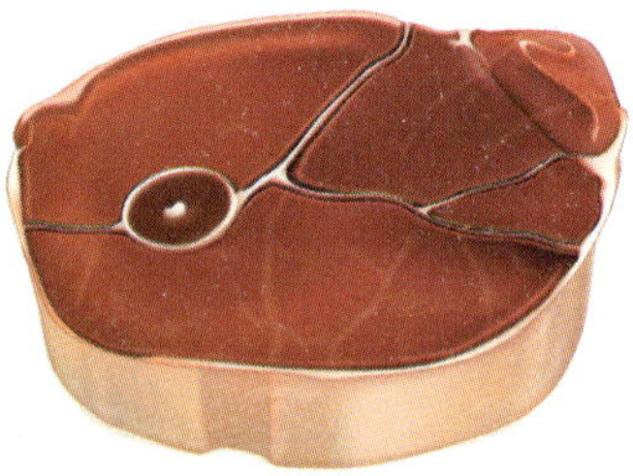

Meat

Egg

Popcorn

Corn

Carrot

Soft drink

Bread

Milk

Date: ________________

Teacher's Signature: ________________

HEALTHY FOOD

Colour the healthy food items and cross the junk food items.

Date: ________________   Teacher's Signature: ________________

PICTURE PASTING

Set your plate with healthy food by pasting pictures.

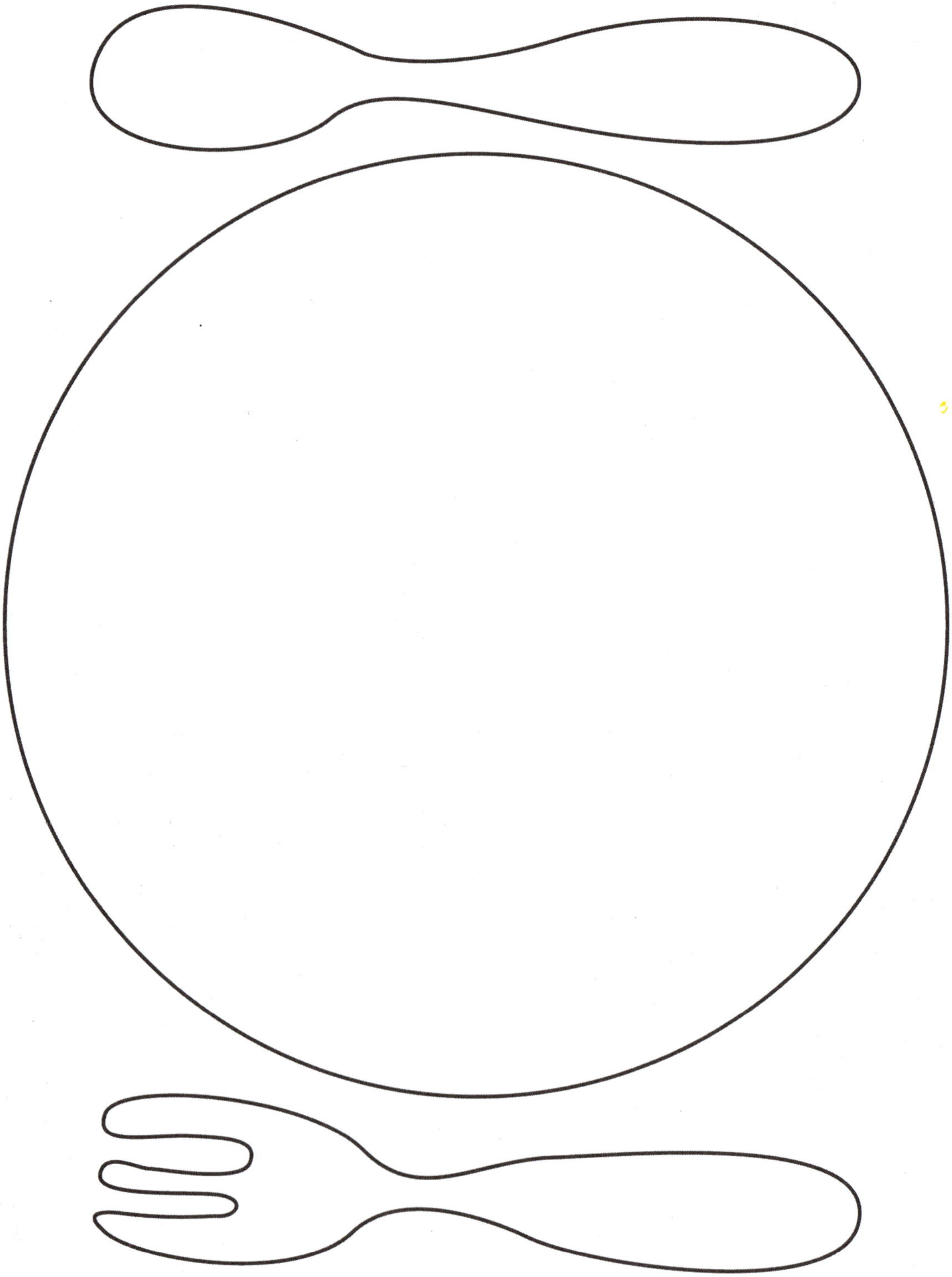

Date: ____________

Teacher's Signature: ____________

COLOUR THE APRON

I must wear an apron when I eat.

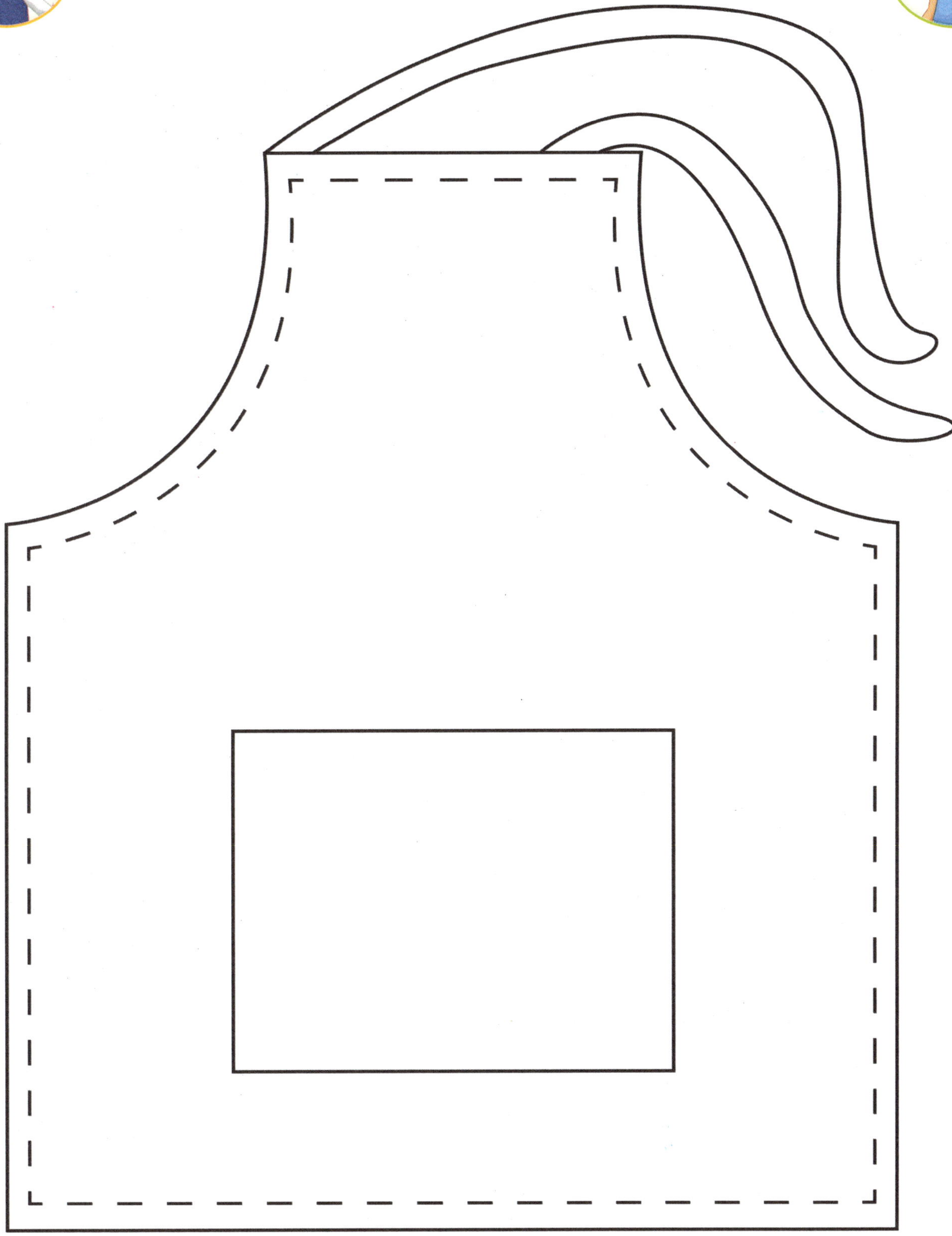

Date: ____________________ Teacher's Signature: ____________________

KNOW YOUR FOOD

Complete the following answers and know your food.

Q1. Are pizza and burger healthy food or junk food?

Ans. Pizza and burger are ____________________

Q2. Name two healthy food items.

Ans. ____________________

Q3. Name two junk foods.

Ans. ____________________

Q4. Paste three pictures of junk food.

Ans.

Date: ____________ Teacher's Signature: ____________

MENU OF THE DAY

Draw/Paste pictures of what you eat.

Morning

Afternoon

Night

Date: ____________________

Teacher's Signature: ____________________

PLANTS AND TREES AROUND US

We see different types of plants around us, like: beautiful flowers, big and tall trees, etc. Plants are very useful to us.

Flowers are of many beautiful colours. Most flowers smell very sweet. We use flowers for decoration and worship.

Trees are tall, big and strong plants. They give us shade, fruits and wood.

Date: ________________ Teacher's Signature: ________________

BEAUTIFUL FLOWERS

Have you seen these flowers?
Colour the flowers.

lotus

rose

daisy

marigold

Date: ________________

Teacher's Signature: ________________

USEFUL PLANTS

Colour the things that we get from plants.

Date: ______________ Teacher's Signature: ______________

TREES AND PLANTS

Paste the pictures of four things that we get from plants and trees.

Date: ______________

Teacher's Signature: ______________

FRUITS AND VEGETABLES

Fruits and Vegetables help us grow strong and healthy.

Most fruits are sweet, fleshy and juicy. Some fruits have stones in them. Fruits are eaten mostly raw.

Green vegetables are good for health. We mostly cook them before we eat them. But we eat some vegetables raw too.

Date: ____________________ Teacher's Signature: ____________________

MY FRUIT BOWL

Help me make my fruit bowl
by colouring the fruits.

Date: ________________ Teacher's Signature: ________________

MY VEGETABLE BOWL

Help me make my vegetable bowl by colouring the vegetables.

Date: ________________ Teacher's Signature: ________________

FRUITS AND VEGETABLES

Complete the following answers and know your fruits and vegetables.

Q1. Name your favourite fruit.

Ans. My favourite fruit is ______________________________

Q2. Name the fruit in the picture.

Ans. This is ______________

Q3. Name any two fruits.

Ans. ____

Q4. Name any two vegetables.

Ans. ____

Q5. What does a monkey eat?

Ans. A monkey eats ____________________

Q6. What does a rabbit eat?

Ans. A rabbit eats ______________________

Q7. Name your favourite vegetable?

Ans. My favourite vegetable is ___________________________

Date: ______________ Teacher's Signature: ______________

I LOVE FRUITS!

Colour the fruits that you like to eat.

Date: ________________ Teacher's Signature: ________________

VEGETABLES MAKE US HEALTHY!

Colour the vegetables.

Date: ________________

Teacher's Signature: ________________

FRUIT BASKET

Paste pictures of your favourite fruits in the basket.

Date: ____________

Teacher's Signature: ____________

USEFUL VEHICLES

Vehicles help us to move from place to place. They are called means of transport. These are the different types of land transport.

Bus

Car

Bicycle

Scooter

Van

Date: ________________ Teacher's Signature: ________________

AIR TRANSPORT

Planes, helicopters and hot air balloons are forms of air transport.

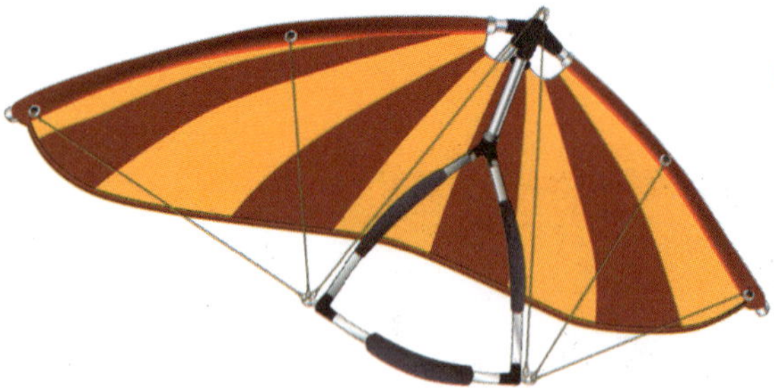

Glider

Aeroplane

Helicopter

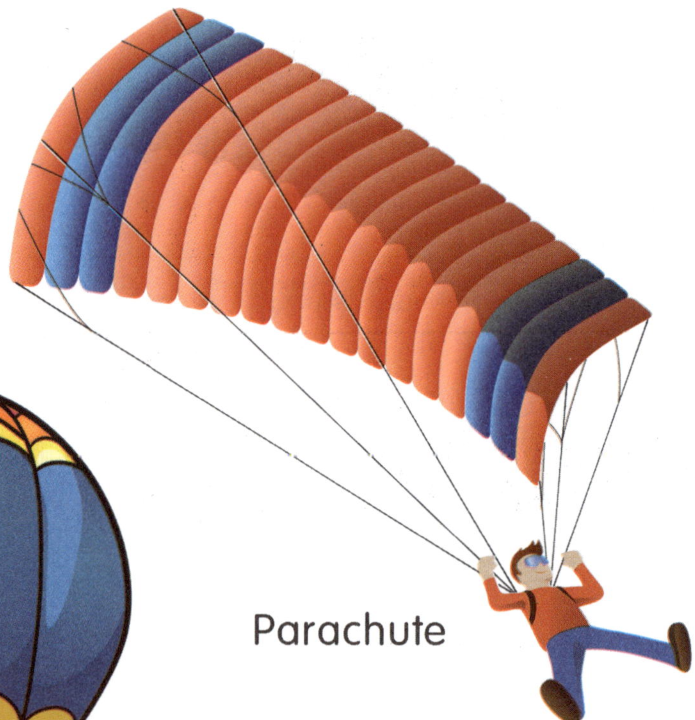

Parachute

Hot Air Balloon

Date: ________________

Teacher's Signature: ________________

WATER TRANSPORT

Ferries, boats, yacht and ships are forms of water transport.

Ship

Yacht

Boat

Date: ________________ Teacher's Signature: ________________

ENCIRCLE AND COLOUR THE VEHICLES WE SEE ON LAND.

Bus

Truck

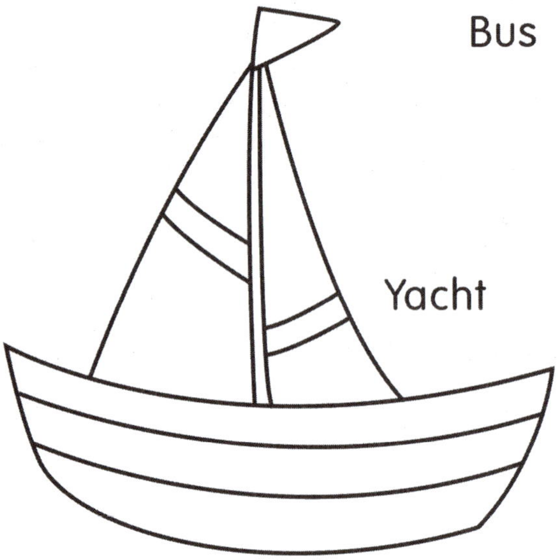

Yacht

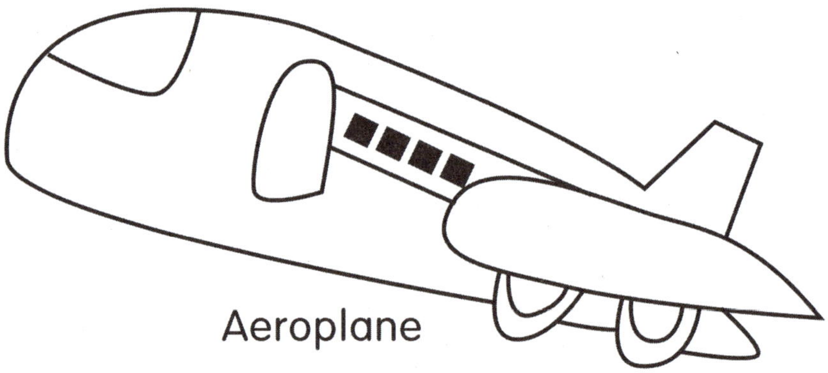

Aeroplane

Van

Car

Date: ________________

Teacher's Signature: ________________

MATCH THE FOLLOWING

Date: ____________________ Teacher's Signature: ____________________

LET US DRAW!

Draw a boat and paste it in the water.

Date: ________________ Teacher's Signature: ________________

MEANS OF TRANSPORT

Complete the following answers to know the means of transport.

Q1. Name the fastest means of transport.

Ans. The fastest means of transport is ____________________

Q2. How do you come to school?

Ans. I come to school by/on ____________________

Q3. What is the colour of your school bus?

Ans. The colour of my school bus is ____________________

Q4. Name any two vehicles of

Ans. Land Transport ____________________

Air Transport ____________________

Water Transport ____________________

Q5. Paste a picture of your school bus.

Ans.

Date: ____________ Teacher's Signature: ____________

THE ANIMAL WORLD

Some animals are very useful to us. Some of them give us milk and some give wool. Some animals work for us and on we ride on, some of them.

frog

goat

duck

sheep

donkey

horse

Date: ______________ Teacher's Signature: ______________

DOMESTIC ANIMALS

We keep some animals such as cows, buffaloes, hens and horses at our farm or around our houses. These are called domestic animals.

Date: ____________________ Teacher's Signature: ____________________

WILD ANIMALS

There are animals which live in the forests and jungles. They are called wild animals.

fox

tiger

elephant

giraffe

lion

bear

Date: ________________   Teacher's Signature: ________________

WATER ANIMALS

Some animals like dolphin, fish, shark, turtle, jellyfish and lobster live in water. They are called water animals.

Date: ________________

Teacher's Signature: ________________

ANIMALS

Colour the domestic animals in green and the wild animals in red.

Date: ____________________

Teacher's Signature: ____________________

LET US VISIT A ZOO

Colour these animals.

Date: ______________

Teacher's Signature: ______________

MATCHING IS FUN!

Match the animals with their shadows.

Date: ____________________

Teacher's Signature: ____________________

THE ANIMAL WORLD

Complete the following answers to know the animal world.

Q1. Which animal lives in water?

Ans. The ________________ lives in water.

Q2. Name any two

Ans. Domestic Animals ________________________________

Water Animals ________________________________

Wild Animals ________________________________

Q3. Which animal gives milk?

Ans. The ______________ gives milk.

Q4. What do we get from sheep?

Ans. The sheep give us ________________________________

Q5. Paste a picture of your favourite animal.

Ans.

Date: ____________ Teacher's Signature: ____________

WE WEAR CLOTHES

We all wear different clothes to cover our body. Cotton clothes are worn during summer and woollen clothes are worn during winter. When it rains we use raincoats and umbrellas.

Shorts

T-Shirt

Shirt

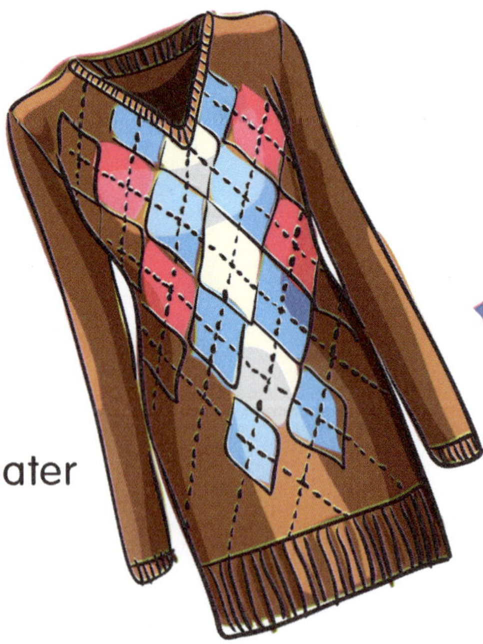

Sweater

Socks

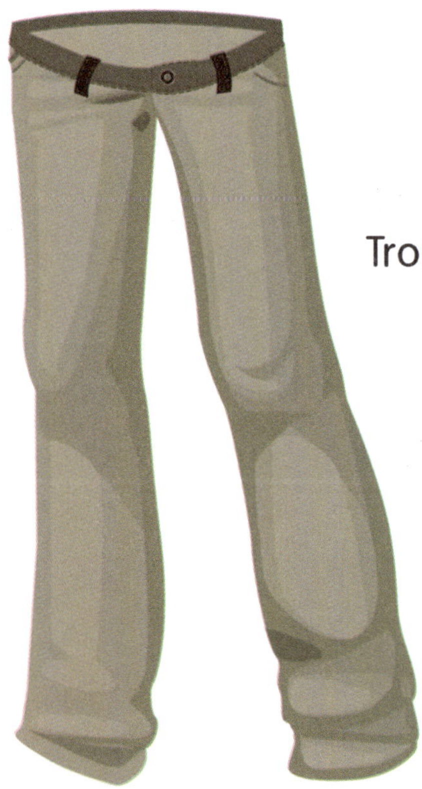

Trouser

Date: ________________

Teacher's Signature: ________________

CLOTHES WE WEAR

T-shirt

Jacket

Frock

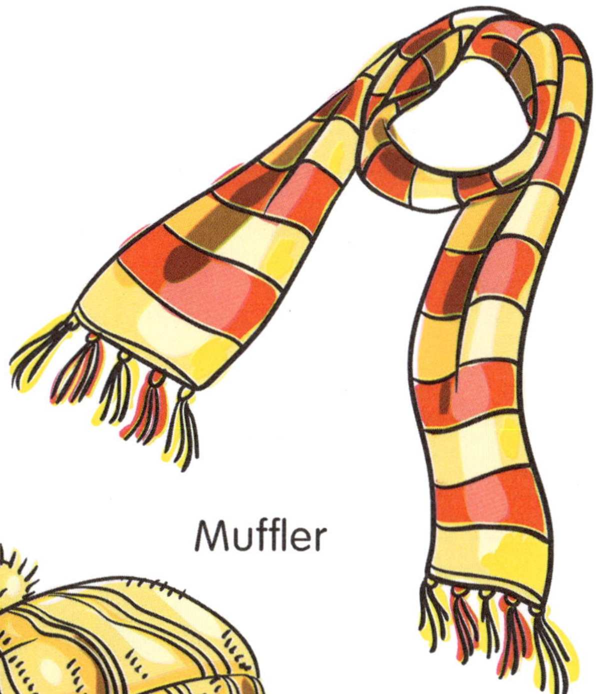

Muffler

Cap

Date: ________________ Teacher's Signature: ________________

PASTING PICTURE

Paste the pictures of clothes you wear in the summer season.

Date: ____________

Teacher's Signature: ____________

MATCHING IS FUN!

When do you wear these clothes?

Monsoon

Winter

Summer

Date: ________________ Teacher's Signature: ________________

COLOUR THE SUMMER CLOTHES BLUE AND THE WINTER CLOTHES RED

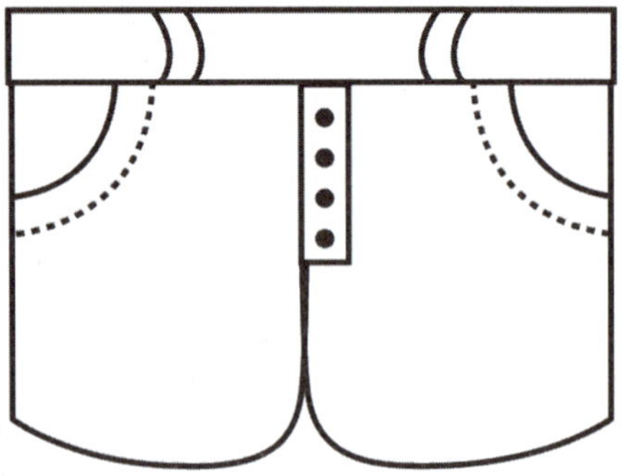

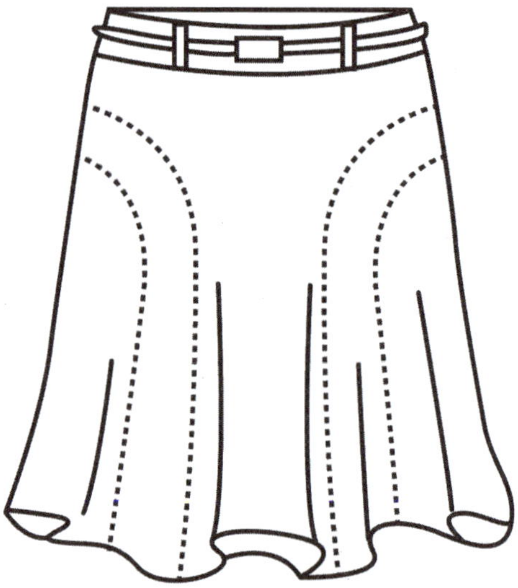

Date: ____________________

Teacher's Signature: ____________________

SEASONS

There are four seasons:
Spring, Summer, Autumn and Winter.

Spring: Spring is a time when plants and trees wake up after a long winters nap.

Summer: Summers have long, hot days. We can wear shorts, slippers and sunglasses.

Autumn: During Autumn time the leaves change to yellow, orange, and red and start to fall off the trees.

Winter: Winter is cold. Children dress warmly to play in the snow.

Date: ________________

Teacher's Signature: ________________

THE SUMMER SEASON

Colour the picture brightly.

Date: ________________ Teacher's Signature: ________________

THE RAINY SEASON

Colour the picture brightly.

Date: ____________________

Teacher's Signature: ____________________

THE WINTER SEASON

Colour the picture brightly.

Date: ______________ Teacher's Signature: ______________

SUMMER TIME

Colour the pictures that belong to the summer season.

Date: ________________ Teacher's Signature: ________________

PASTE PITURES RELATED TO DIFFERENT SEASONS

Summer 	
Winter 	
Rainy 	

Date: ______________ Teacher's Signature: ______________

OUR HELPERS

These are the people who help us.

Doctor

Chef

Fireman

Painter

Date: ____________

Teacher's Signature: ____________

OUR HELPERS

These are the people who help us.

Policeman

Postman

Nurse

Farmer

Teacher

Date: ______________

Teacher's Signature: ______________

DO YOU KNOW?

Match the helpers with their activities.

Doctor

Painter

Policeman

Fireman

Date: ________________ Teacher's Signature: ________________

MATCHING FUN!

Match the helpers with their belongings.

Date: ________________

Teacher's Signature: ________________

KNOW YOUR HELPERS

Complete the following answers to know your helpers.

Q1. Who delivers the letters to us?

Ans. The ________________ delivers letters to us.

Q2. Who brings milk for us?

Ans. The ________________ brings milk for us.

Q3. Who guards our house?

Ans. The ________________ guards our house.

Q4. To whom do we go when we are sick?

Ans. We go to the ________________ when we are sick.

Q5. Who teaches us?

Ans. The ________________ teaches us.

Q6. Who cooks food for us?

Ans. The ________________ cooks food for us.

Q7. Who catches thieves?

Ans. The ________________ catches thieves.

Date: ________________ Teacher's Signature: ________________

KNOW THE COLOURS

We see many colours around us.
Here are the objects of the colour **RED**.

Apple

Tomato

Cherry

Watermelon

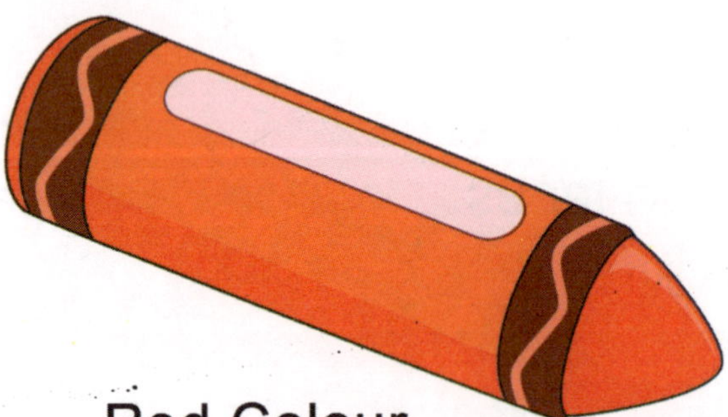

Red Colour

Ladybug

Date: ________________   Teacher's Signature: ________________

KNOW THE COLOURS

We see many colours around us.
Here are the objects of the colour **BLUE**.

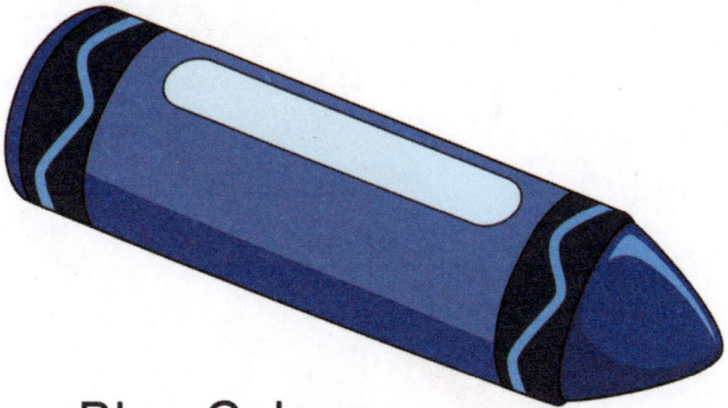

Blue Colour

Balloon

Car

Shirt

Flower

Blueberries

Date: ______________

Teacher's Signature: ______________

KNOW THE COLOURS

We see many colours around us.
Here are the objects of the colour **ORANGE**.

Orange

Carrot

Pumpkin

Fish

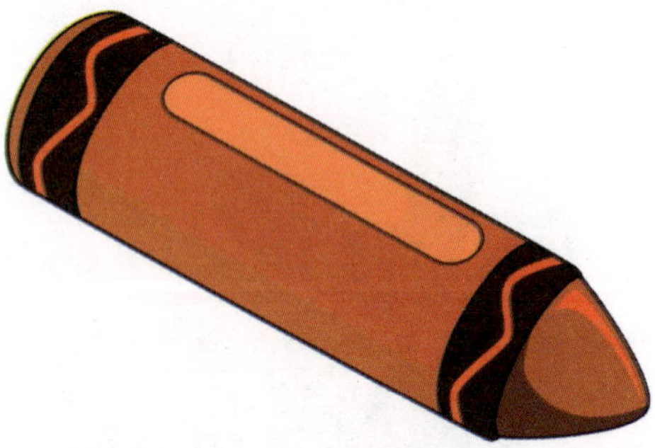

Orange Colour

Flower

Date: ______________ Teacher's Signature: ______________

KNOW THE COLOURS

We see many colours around us.
Here are the objects of the colour **GREEN**.

Parrot

Capsicum

Cucumber

Pear

Leaf

Grapes

Date: ________________

Teacher's Signature: ________________

KNOW THE COLOURS

We see many colours around us.
Here are the objects of the colour **YELLOW**.

Yellow Colour

Duck

Banana

Mango

Sun

Flower

Date: ________________ Teacher's Signature: ________________

PASTE TWO GREEN COLOURED OBJECTS

PASTE TWO YELLOW COLOURED OBJECTS

Date: ____________________

Teacher's Signature: ____________________

PASTE TWO RED COLOURED OBJECTS

PASTE TWO BLUE COLOURED OBJECTS

Date: ______________ Teacher's Signature: ______________